Happy
30TH
Birthday

Happy 30th Birthday

A Book of Wit and Wisdom

Edited by Mary Rodarte

Illustrated by Tammy Smith

Ariel Books

Andrews McMeel Publishing

Kansas City

 For information write Andrews McMeel Publishing, an Andrews McMeel Universal company, 4520 Main Street, Kansas City, Missouri 64111.

www.andrewsmcmeel.com

ISBN: 0-8362-7886-0
Library of Congress Catalog Card Number: 98-86358

Contents

Happy
30TH
Birthday

Introduction

Happy birthday! You're thirty years old and you stand at the border of uncharted terrain.

Many goals begin with the words, "By the time I'm thirty. . . ." You may have reached those goals easily or with great effort, but either way, the thirtieth year is a milestone in our lives—a year, to many, of accountability and achievement.

Perhaps you have just finished

college, or you've just returned to school. You may have started a family, or decided a roommate is all you can handle for now. Your career might be rewarding and successful, or perhaps this is the year to go for that job you've always dreamed of. At whatever stage you are in life, turning thirty is many things, but rarely is it uneventful.

So as you celebrate this special

birthday, whether quietly or with a bang, take time to look back on the events that have made you who you are this day. Read this book and enjoy the humor and wisdom of those who have gone before you. And remember: Whatever lies ahead, you have the knowledge and experience of thirty years to see you through it.

Life after 29

Never trust a woman who will not lie about her age after thirty. She is unwomanly and unhuman, and there is no knowing what crimes she will commit.

—Gertrude Atherton

After thirty, a body has a mind of its own.

—Bette Midler

When you turn thirty, a whole new thing happens: You see yourself acting like your parents.

—Blair Sabol

At twenty years of age, the will reigns; at thirty, the wit; at forty, the judgment.

—Benjamin Franklin

At thirty, man suspects himself
a fool;
Knows it at forty, and reforms
his plan . . .

—Edward Young

Another belief of mine: that everyone else my age is an adult, whereas I am merely in disguise.

—Margaret Atwood

The aging aren't only the old; the aging are all of us.

—Alexandra Robbin

It's not how old you are but how you are old.

—Marie Dressler

I grow more intense as I age.

—Florida Scott-Maxwell

You grow up the day you have your first real laugh—at yourself.

—Ethel Barrymore

It is lovely, when I forget all birth-days, including my own, to find that somebody remembers me.

—Ellen Glasgow

A new year is a clean slate, a chance to suck in your breath, decide all is not lost, and give yourself another chance.

—Sarah Overstreet

I have no romantic feelings about age. Either you are interesting at any age or you are not. There is nothing particularly interesting about being old—or being young for that matter.

—Katharine Hepburn

Man arrives as a novice at each age of his life.

—Nicolas Chamfort

What he hath scanted men in hair,
he hath given them in wit.

—William Shakespeare

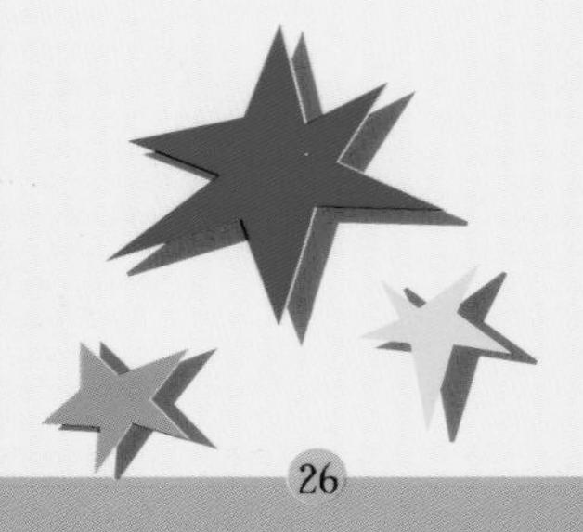

All the humiliating, tragicomic, heartbreaking things happened to me in my girlhood, and nothing makes me happier than to realize I cannot possibly relive my youth.

—Ilka Chase

At eighteen, one adores at once; at twenty, one loves; at thirty, one desires; at forty, one reflects.

—Paul de Kock

Age is something that doesn't matter, unless you are a cheese.

—Billie Burke

Youth supplies us with the colors,
age with canvas.

—Henry David Thoreau

H A P P Y
No wise man ever wished to be younger.
—Jonathan Swift

At ten, a child; at twenty, wild;
At thirty, tame if ever;
At forty, wise; at fifty, rich;
At sixty, good, or never.

—Anonymous

Gifts for the
Thirtieth
Birthday

A thirty-day trial membership to a gym

A round-trip ticket to the destination located nearest to thirty degrees latitude and thirty degrees longitude—Cairo, Egypt

A tennis bracelet with thirty diamond chips on it

A list of thirty things to love about you

A thirty-day pass to the local zoo, museum, or aquarium

A bottle of thirty-year-old wine

Thirty hours of flying lessons

A thirty-inch sub sandwich

A leather-bound journal and a Mont Blanc pen

A globe and the number of a good travel agent

Eat, Drink,
and Be Merry

Curiosity is a gift, a capacity of pleasure in knowing, which if you destroy, you make yourselves cold and dull.

—John Ruskin

The first hundred years are the hardest.

—Wilson Mizner

Youth comes but once in a lifetime.

—Henry Wadsworth Longfellow

You stay young as long as you can learn, acquire new habits, and suffer contradiction.

—Marie von Ebner-Eschenbach

It's a very short trip.

While alive, live.

—Malcolm Forbes

The hardest years in life are those between ten and seventy.

—Helen Hayes

In this country, some people start being miserable about growing old while they are still young.

—Margaret Mead

Youth is not a time of life—it is a state of mind. . . . Youth means a temperamental predominance of courage over timidity, of the appetite for adventure over a life of ease. . . .

—Samuel Ullman

Everything I did in my life that was worthwhile I caught hell for.

—Earl Warren

The great pleasure in life is doing what people say you cannot do.

—Walter Bagehot

How old would you be if you didn't know how old you was?

—Satchel Paige

He that is not handsome at twenty, nor strong at thirty, nor rich at forty, nor wise at fifty, will never be handsome, strong, rich, or wise.

—George Herbert

It is better to waste one's youth than to do nothing with it at all.

—George Courteline

Each age, like every individual, has its own characteristic intoxication.

—Will Durant

There's only one thing worse than an old fogey, and that's a young fogey.

—Terrell Bell

Live your life and forget your age.

—Frank Bering

Her birthdays were always important to her; for being a born lover of life, she would always keep the day of her entrance into it as a very great festival indeed.

—Elizabeth Goudge

One today is worth two tomorrows.

—Benjamin Franklin

Youth is happy because it has the ability to see beauty. Anyone who keeps the ability to see beauty never grows old.

—Franz Kafka

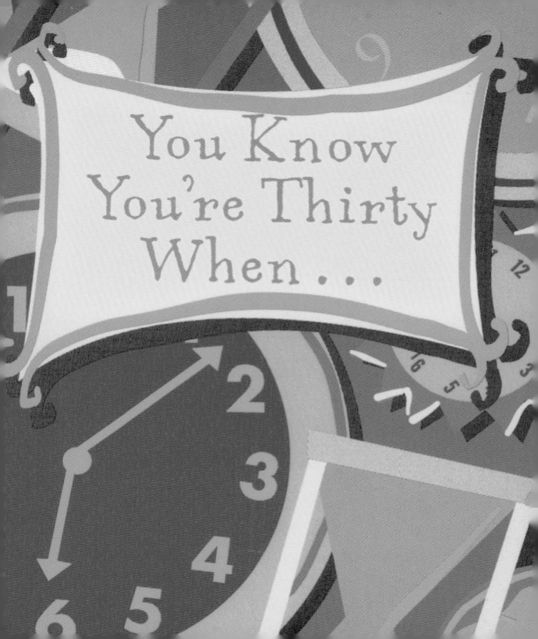
You Know
You're Thirty
When . . .

People suddenly start discussing your biological clock

You don't know the price of a keg of beer

You pay a mortgage rather than rent

You actually know what's going on in the Middle East

You find yourself disgusted at the way kids drive these days

You feel nostalgic when you hear U2's "Sunday, Bloody Sunday" on the radio

You don't know who Jenny McCarthy is, and you're pretty sure you don't care

You remember when Christie Brinkley was a supermodel

You're dismayed at the violence on TV

You'd rather spend your paycheck on good furniture than good beer

You finally own more ties than shot glasses

You are religious about seeing the dentist every six months

You pay for your parents when you all go out to dinner

You develop a fear of flying, driving too fast, and swimming alone

groovy

Your elementary school lunch box is considered a collector's item

The amount of your school loan no longer makes you burst into tears or laughter

You stop saying, "By the time I'm thirty . . ."

Looking
Ahead

Youth is, after all, just a moment,
but it is the moment, the spark that
you always carry in your heart.

—Raisa M. Gorbachev

I'd like to grow very old as slowly
as possible.

—Irene Mayer Selznick

When you realize the value of all life, you dwell less on what is past and concentrate more on the preservation of the future.

—Dian Fossey

Our grand business undoubtedly is not to see what lies dimly at a distance, but to do what lies clearly at hand.

—Thomas Carlyle

There is no good reason why we should not develop and change until the last day we live.

—Karen Horney

SURPRISE

Age only matters when one is aging. Now that I have arrived at a great age, I might just as well be twenty.

—Pablo Picasso

We must use time as a tool, not as a couch.

—John F. Kennedy

The belief that youth is the happiest time of life is founded upon a fallacy. The happiest person is the person who thinks the most interesting thoughts, and we grow happier as we grow older.

—William Lyon Phelps

The process of maturing is an art to be learned, an effort to be sustained.

—Mayra Mannes

Try to keep your soul young and quivering right up to old age.

—George Sand

May all your future years be
Free from disappointment, care,
or strife,
That every birthday you will be
A little more in love with life.

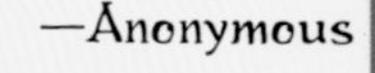

—Anonymous

Nothing is more rewarding than the effort a man makes to matter—to count, to stand for something, to have it make some difference that he lived at all.

—Leo Rosten

If you don't learn to laugh at trouble, you won't have anything to laugh at when you grow old.

—Ed Howe

Life can only be understood backwards; but it must be lived forwards.

—Søren Kierkegaard

Tomorrow is the most important thing in life. Comes into us at midnight very clean. It's perfect when it arrives and it puts itself in our hands. It hopes we've learned something from yesterday.

—John Wayne

Resolve to be tender with the young, compassionate with the aged, sympathetic with the striving, and tolerant with the weak and the wrong. Sometime in life you will have been all of these.

—Bob Goddard

It is never too late to be what you might have been.

—George Eliot

The text of this book is set
in Aunt Mildred and Steam
by Mspace, Katonah, New York.

Book design
by Maura Fadden Rosenthal